R·E·M·E·M·B·E·R·I·N·G· M·A·T·T·H·E·W· P·E·R·R·Y·

By

Darlene

SCAN THIS QR CODE TO JOIN MY GROUP.

MEMORIES

Acknowledgments

Thank you for making this all possible and your never-ending support. Stacy and Casey Hackbarth, Krista and Sydney Roberts, Leslie Hood, Ned and Brenda Bissett, Marla Jefferys, and Cosette Wright. All departments of Global Publishing. Countless Matthew Perry Fans and Matthew Perry, himself.

About the Author

Darlene Beasecker, a first-time author, has written a book for all the faithful fans of Matthew Perry. She has kept a diary, noting the grieving process. The diary has been kept and shared with Matty's fans through social media. She has decided to put all her entries into words to share her thoughts and memories as a loving fan.

Darlene is a widow of two years and newly retired. She cares for her family dearly since they are a close-knit family. The hope is that this story helps you, the reader, with your grieving process. Matthew had a huge fan base in life and now in death, who she hopes to reach with this book. She hopes for it to bring help and comfort to those dealing with the passing of our beloved Matty.

Dedication

This book is dedicated to:

Matthew's Family and "Friends" friends

To the memory of Michael, my beloved husband.

To Matthew Langford Perry, who brought so much joy to this world that it will never be the same.

October 25, 2023

"I think this is probably why Dimon smokes in his cell alone."

That's what he says and tricks the gullible Joey into giving him a cigarette. It is a rainy afternoon; the blowing winds and droplets of rain have created a great atmosphere. In weather like this, one loves to snuggle inside the covers and drink something hot to keep warm. Basically, a person wants to be as comfortable and relaxed as humanly possible. My rainy day routine was no different than others. With a hastily made hot chocolate, I was sitting on my couch with a blanket to protect me from the bone-chilling wind. I was watching a rerun of FRIENDS.

There he was, standing in his light blue shirt; he took a cigarette from Joey to teach him how to smoke. Gracefully, he takes a drag. This image has been burned into my mind: his medium-length brown hair, blue eyes, and perfect smile. I first saw this handsome man back in 1994 and have been captivated ever since. The man in question is Matthew Perry. Some might only know him as Chandler Bing from FRIENDS or the funny guy from Friends.

My love for this man goes beyond that. This particular scene has been etched inside the part of my brain where everything I love resides. Oh, how I wish I could meet him one day. I'll sign off now. It's time to sleep. I hope he visits me in my dreams tonight like he has several times before. I heard that the people you think about or interact with before going to bed are more likely to be present in your dreams as they are still part of your subconscious mind. I try to practice this as much as I can. Before going to bed, I go through some edits and pictures of Matthew to increase the likelihood of him appearing in my dreams. Let's see what happens tonight, but for that, I would like to shut my eyes first.

October 26, 2023

I've just woken up. Guess what? He returned last night! He really did; I remember it clearly. After signing off from here, I started surfing my socials and entertained myself with the numerous edits online. I remember putting my phone away when it slipped out of my hand and onto my face. Here I was, sitting on the iconic orange couch, drinking coffee.

The door of the café opens, which is notified by the soft ding of the bell attached to it. I turn my head to see him in all his glory. There he stands in era-appropriate baggy jeans and a black sweatshirt, the national attire of the 90s. The man standing there was not Chandler Bing but very much Matthew Perry appearing as himself. His grey beard and disheveled hair against this background made him look like a character from one of the Back to the Future movies. He looks around the crowd, and suddenly, his icy blue eyes get fixated on me.

His eyes were one of his features that had withstood the test of time. The brightness they had within them had been consistent despite the ups and downs of life. When I say ups and downs, I really mean it. If he had gone through any more, he could very easily give the escalators a run for their money. (Matty would be proud of this one. If only I could tell him this one in person.)

He starts moving towards the couch. I could feel his gaze, not in a creepy way, but in a way that the hot chocolate yesterday made me feel all warm and cozy from the inside out. This man, swaggering forward, mesmerized me. It felt as if he was the only person in the café. The path from the door to the couch was mere steps, but it felt as if the more he moved, the more the path stretched out. Starting to get impatient, I got up and started running (this is what confirmed my belief that it was a dream). I reached up to Matty and hugged him tightly.

The constraints of time and space melted away as I hugged him for God knows how long. (Although my pillow felt the intensity of my embrace as it had gotten disfigured—the filling had been divided into pieces, leaving a massive divot in the middle.) I then let go of Matty. Still staring into his eyes, I thanked him for everything he had done, thanked him for existing. (I don't care how cheesy it sounded because it was coming from a place of love.) He patiently heard my words, smiling.

Ahhh, his smile... His smile made his face shine. His smile was a genuine one; it was effortless, it was something else. This was no PR agency exercise, run-of-the-mill smile.

"Darlene, the pleasure is all mine. Thank you for not giving up on me."

Matty said those exact words to me. A jolt of energy ran through me when I heard my name out of his mouth. He had appeared in my dreams a handful of times. However, never had he been so direct with me. His appearances previously had been sporadic. The most common one was where I was sitting by a café, and he would often appear alone, sometimes with a *friend* or all of them. He would pass by me, oblivious to the fact that I was right there with my mouth open in awe of him. It felt as if I was looking through a looking glass or was invisible to them.

More often than not, my dreams would take me to Monica's apartment, where it felt as if I was a member of the crew watching Matty interact with his co-stars. There were some peculiar ones as well. In one of my odd dreams, my conscience had been transferred to the fountain in front of which (later around) the gang danced in the opening scene. (I know, extremely weird.) In another one, I am a 6th grader sitting in the back of the class of the Inner Harlem School, and Mr. Ron Clark comes into the class and starts teaching. Could that be any weirder? (See what I did!)

Coming to the original point, never have I ever had an intimate moment like that with Matty in my dreams until now. I think this encounter with him truly means something; maybe it is the universe's way of telling me that I will be meeting him sooner than later.

What has fate in store for Matty and me? Only time will tell. Maybe I'm getting too ahead of myself. After all, it's just a silly little dream that I'm probably thinking of too much. But it sure would be nice to meet him for real. My Gosh, I've just glanced at the clock. It turns out that I have been writing for like an hour or so. I can write a lot more about the fantastic encounter that I had with Matty, but other matters need my attention (Unfortunately). I am signing off right now; I may or may not write later.

October 27, 2023

October is coming to an end; the fall season is going on in its full effect. I have been on the lookout for the perfect Jack o Lantern. The trick is to buy them a day or two before. I love carving them and placing them outside my house. I live for the trick-or-treaters; their cute costumes warm my heart.

I have a busy day ahead. I will visit a pumpkin patch and then go to the store to buy candies for the kids and decorations. I wonder how Matty spends his Halloween. Does he also carve Jack o Lanterns and set up candy baskets for the trick-or-treaters? Knowing him, he might have been more inclined to trick them first. I can see him smiling, laughing, admiring the aftermath of his foolproof plan, his bright blue eyes shining. He would treat them, too, because he's a kind soul. I want to see him in person for once. I am just dying to do it. The beautiful sensation I felt in the dream yesterday. I want to feel it with my eyes open. Here's to wishful thinking!

There, I start again with the daydreaming. A lot has to be done today I must focus! I am signing off for now but will write once I come back.

10:00

I returned around seven at the house, freshened up, and took care of some chores. While fixing up dinner, an idea struck me. Why don't I watch the Halloween episode today? I love to see Matty in a pink bunny costume. I wore a similar outfit to one of the Halloween parties in my early years. So it began I watched the said episode. Ate dinner, prayed, and now I'm going to sleep.

October 28, 2023

It is a beautiful morning, I woke up today and saw the sun was out. Sadly, Matty didn't appear in my dream last night. As a matter of fact, I didn't dream much at all. This seems a little peculiar to me. No matter how tired I am, I usually dream. Whether it be a random one like seeing a beach or a field or a specific one I had the other night, my dreams are part of my sleep routine. Maybe I'm overstressing over nothing. I will prepare the pumpkins to carve for Halloween night today. I will also prepare the decorations today. Fingers crossed, the children don't TP or egg my house.

9:00 pm

Oh, what has happened? I feel like screaming and crying simultaneously, but shock prevails over all those emotions. I am numbed out, almost paralyzed by the sadness. My dear Matty is no more. How could this be? I just saw you in my dream a day ago. You were happy and smiling. Was that a signal that you had given? I think it was; never had you ever addressed me by my name. I had always been an extra in my own dream with all the spotlight on you. Oh, Matty, why did you have to go? I feel like a piece of my heart has been ripped away from me.

Only once have I felt such intense feelings before that was when Michael (May he Rest in Peace) died. I still remember to this day how devastated I was. Michael or Mike was a great person, the greatest husband a woman could ask for. Just like Matty, Mike had a wonderful smile. I remember when we would go out or picnic, and he would always look at me and smile so charmingly that my heart would melt just by looking at him.

He was always the life of the party, incredibly understanding and caring. He was one of those people who was comfortable with himself; his confidence and overall security as a man-made him so desirable to me. He knew about my obsession with Matty but never felt insecure about my feelings. A lesser man in his place would have gone crazy. This made me fall deeper in love with that man.

I remember when Mike and I were in the living room watching an episode of F.R.I.E.N.D.S., and he joked that Mathew could have you all for himself when I am gone. Until then, he'll have to put up a tough fight. Fate has played me a sick hand in the space of two and a half years, both of you have left me to join in heaven. Leaving me all to myself. I feel all the energy within me seeping out.

I heard about the news around 5, thinking surely this might be one of the Halloween shenanigans of the trolls, even though I was extremely triggered by it. After a while, my phone went off due to the countless notifications of the fan pages I followed. Alas, it is true. After that, the floodgates opened. I was shaking uncontrollably. The tears started flowing automatically. Since then, I've been lying in the bed face down. Your book has just arrived via mail. I had opened it up. I see your glowing face on my nightstand. I am still pinching myself hard, continuously praying that it's just a nightmare. I realized it had been 4 hours since I lay in bed and stared at the roof. Not knowing what I would do without you.

It was quite compelling to me how much you mean in my life. I had never met you. Neither had seen you in the real world. All of our interactions had been through a screen. But still, your tragic demise affected me in such a drastic manner. The details are now being circulated in the media.

They say the authorities found you submerged in your hot tub where they couldn't resuscitate you. This broke my heart into smithereens. Your memories will remain with your fans forever. No matter what happens. Even if the world forgets (though that is Impossible), I will always remember you. You will stay in my heart forever.

October 29ᵗʰ, 2023

I barely slept yesterday. I closed my eyes, but to no avail. I picked up my phone and started scrolling after an hour or so. Then I opened my laptop and started watching a random episode of F.R.I.E.N.D.S. Doing so had been a part of my bedtime routine.

There he was, dancing and prancing. Watching Matty laughing and interacting with his other cast members warmed my heart. I had developed a habit of falling asleep watching Friends (Matty in particular). Yesterday was no different at all. The episodes doubled last night, as I missed him more than usual. Another reason might be that I really wanted him to visit me in my dream.

Well, what I was doing was quite paradoxical to what I wanted. I should have slept earlier after watching an episode or two. That would've given me enough hours to sleep and would have increased his probability of appearing. I was not thinking straight at that time. I was mourning my precious Matty. Anyway, it was 5:00 in the morning when I finally dozed off. It is currently 9 in the morning.

I just realized I had spent 12 hours in the bed. I had promised myself to be as active as I could be. I mean, I love relaxing as much as the next person does. However, I have set a standard for myself and have been adamant in following that. Oh, Matty, your demise dealt me such a blow that my resilience went out the door. Let's keep it till here. I'll write more later.

8:00 pm

I had some chores to do around the house. I did those and now I am free. I figured I should get some writing done. I watched the news, and there he was. They had attached a relatively recent picture of Matty. He was wearing a light blue T-shirt with relaxed black pants.

His hair has always been one of my favorite features. He looked good in whatever he did with it. His salt-and-pepper hair and beard made him look extremely handsome. But what took the cake were the stylish tinted glasses he was wearing. It put the whole look together. Even though it hid his baby blues, he looked extremely dashing. The headline that ran beneath was not.

FRIENDS STAR MATTHEW PERRY FOUND DEAD AT HIS LA RESIDENCE.

Several celebrities have paid tribute to you, but I have not heard anything from your "friends." I think they are as hurt as me, shocked beyond their senses. While surfing through my socials, I came across the tweet that The President of Canada had written about you.

Matthew Perry's passing is shocking and saddening. I'll never forget the schoolyard games we used to play, and I know people around the world are never going to forget the joy he brought them. Thanks for all the laughs, Matthew. You were loved – and you will be missed.

— Justin Trudeau (@JustinTrudeau) October 29, 2023

I remember watching your interview; it was one of those late-night shows. You were wearing a suit, clean-shaven, and black spectacles. Your hair was cut short and styled fashionably. You told them how you and President Trudeau were in the same school.

Moreover, how you and your friend roughed him up. The way you narrated that story was so captivating yet so funny that I watched the whole interview twice (thrice if you count me loading it up right now)

I'll write further tomorrow. I need to watch this right now.

October 30ᵗʰ, 2023

Oh, praise the Lord, the Lord is great. I saw him in my dream. I silently prayed before bed for Matty to appear in my dream. I was sitting in the audience section of a studio. The theater was engulfed in laughter. I was looking around, wondering what they were laughing about. Almost immediately, a wave of silence fell over. Somehow, I knew my arrival had caused the sudden change as I looked around to find answers.

A spotlight, blinding me, was cast upon me. Here I sat befuddled, wondering what was happening. A figure came swaggering towards me. As the spotlight eased on me, I started to see things again. I rubbed my eyes and blinked to adjust to the room's lighting. As I opened my eyes, there he was standing in all his glory, wearing the suit. His piercing stare fixated on me. I couldn't move a muscle trapped in his gaze. He raised his arm toward his mouth, holding a microphone. And he said

"Why, Darlene, didn't you find me beating up my country's President Story funny?

Could it be any more funnier?"

As I was about to say something, laughter erupted around me, then a sequence of applause. He winked at me when my eyes met his. Before I could do anything, he had disappeared in thin air. So did the studio, the crowd, and the spotlight. All that was left was poor Darlene in her bed.

I am over the moon; Matty had appeared again in my dream. I did not know what was in store for me next.

October 31th, 2023

I woke up today and looked right into the eyes of the shabby mess standing in front of the mirror. My eyes were bloodshot and puffier than usual, probably due to all the tears I had shed during the night. Suddenly, the eyes on the other side of the mirror started clearing. The hazel color of my eyes began transforming. It grew lighter and lighter and turned blue. When my eyes moved to the rest of the reflection, I saw hair that was disheveled in a rather fashionable way. The salt and pepper of the hair gave it away.

It was Matty! But what was he doing here? In my house, not long after his demise? He was dressed in an all-black suit that brought out the color in his eyes and contrasted well with his hair. Seeing him turned my body to stone. I could not move a muscle. After a couple of seconds, he looked at me empathetically and smiled.

"How's it going, Darlene? You hang in there, girl. If not for yourself and me, then do it for Mike. Oh, he says hello and seems quite happy to see me for some reason. I don't know why; I cannot seem to put my finger on it."

Just like always, as I was about to say something, a laughter track blared around me, breaking my trance and bringing me back to my senses; as I started to move, I felt my knees buckle. Fortunately, I was near the bed. The last thing I wanted with a broken heart was a fractured hip. I've seen people close to me suffer through both and can't decide which is more painful.

The laughter that brought me back to real life was from my laptop. I watched *F.R.I.E.N.D.S.* the night before, and something must have caused it to play sporadically. When I grabbed the laptop to close it, I saw the screen. *The Last One* was playing.

I decided to watch it. I remembered the first time I saw that episode in '04, when it was initially released. A couple of friends and I organized a cute little watch party to see the episode together. By the end, we were all crying. I remember the very last line of the series when Rachel suggests they have coffee for the last time as a group.

The always-on-point Chandler Bing replies with, "Sure, Where?" Amidst the laughter and cheers, the screen blacks out. The tale ends. I always had a feeling that Matty must have written the last dialogue. He was allowed to sit with the writing team because of his great comedic timing. Later on, I found out that I was right. This dialogue was not included in the script, and Matty just made it up.

As I lay in my bed, his words played repeatedly in my ears: *You hang in there, girl. If not for yourself and me, then do it for Mike.* Matty was pushing me to get a hold of myself. He even told me about Mike in his ever-so-humorous way. After an hour or so of thinking, I got up and started preparing for Halloween. Even though I was in no mood to laugh and have fun, I figured I had to do it. This is what Matty would've done, too.

I did some chores around the house and decorated my driveway with appropriate props. Later on, the kids came. Their cute little costumes brought me some well-needed comfort. Seeing them smile and hearing their laughs proved therapeutic to me. I smiled and joked with the kids and their parents throughout the evening. Matty was right. I need to hang in there. It's about twelve now. I will write more later. I have loaded up the Halloween episode on my laptop. I will watch it now. Fingers crossed, he might appear in my dream today dressed as a bunny.

.

December 25th, 2023

I have been inactive for quite some time. The last time I wrote was all the way back in October. It has been quite challenging for me to write. I haven't forgotten you, Matty. You are always with me in my prayers, dreams, and thoughts. I remember watching the Halloween episode that night. After the episode ended, I just lay there on my bed. Almost involuntarily, I started crying. I have been trying to hold back a lot ever since your death. I just cried a lot. I knew the volatility of life and had always wanted to prepare myself for the event of your demise. However, all that preparation went out the window. I sobbed and wept like a baby.

I watched *The Whole Nine Yards* today. You were so handsome in that movie. Later on, as I was eating dinner, I figured, let's go with a festive theme and watch a Christmas episode. I watched the one where you dressed up as Santa Claus. I have gone through loads of websites researching coping mechanisms. The most prominent and common suggestion I saw was that the healing process is not linear. We all have our unique ways of processing loss. Let's say that seeing you dressed up as Santa in an absurd way helps me process the pain.

I'll write more later. Till then, goodbye, Matty. (May his soul rest in peace.)

December 31st, 2023

It's the last day of the year. A fairly cold day, and the coldness elevates my loneliness. I sit by the window, watching the street and cars passing by. *Friends, Lovers, and the Big Terrible Thing* hardcover sits by me, Matty staring down my soul with his electric blue eyes. After Mike's passing, you have been a constant companion to me. Even though I had not met you formally or physically, you were and still are familiar to me. For a long time, I have wanted to meet you in person to enjoy your pleasant company. This void of emptiness is consuming my happiness.

Oh, Matty, I keep trying to come to terms with your death, but I just cannot. The other day, I went to play bingo with a couple of my friends. Playing bingo in the evening is one of my favorite activities. I rang them up and informed them I would accompany them that day. They were pleased to hear that, as I had been living like a hermit for quite some time.

I was staring at the red, yellow, and blue game pieces during the game. I couldn't help but notice that the pieces resembled the dots between the FRIENDS logo appearing in the opening sequence. Almost immediately, my mind wandered off to the fountain, and I saw Matty dancing awkwardly with his friends. And almost immediately, a smile appeared on my face. A warmth engulfed my body. I felt better after a long time. My gals noticed my flushed red cheeks. I found myself uncharacteristically ecstatic. For once, the sadness had somehow evaporated from my system. We laughed and joked all evening.

Later, we returned to my house and watched the live transmission of the New Year Ceremony. At precisely 11:59, we got up and yelled, "3...2...1...Happy New Year!" in unison. I was a little upset when I thought that neither Mike nor Matty would be present with me this year.

12:40 am

I'm in my bed now. After a memorable evening, I lay in bed and opened my laptop. Doubling down on the wave of happiness that had hit me earlier in the evening, I decided to watch *The One With the Blackout*. I find this episode one of the best of the series. Matty in the first season was stunning, I mean absolutely stunning. In his early 20s, the beginning of his prime years. His long brown hair, dashing smile, and two bolts of electricity were his eyes. There he was, standing in all his glory, wearing a black overcoat, loose-fitted pants (a staple of the '90s), and a powder blue shirt.

He looks so handsome in this ensemble. In my humble opinion, Matty did most of the comedic heavy lifting of this episode, and I absolutely love his dynamic with Jill Goodacre. He played out his shy, socially awkward persona to a T. I laughed out loud when he was mumbling over the phone to inform his friends about being stuck in an ATM vestibule with Jill Goodacre. I'm calling it a night. I feel really spent and want to sleep as soon as possible. There is an inkling of hope that he might visit me tonight.

January 1st, 2024

As my eyes opened, I found myself lying in a chair. The type of chair that had an extendable leg support. A bright white, almost blinding light illuminated in front of my face. I could not make out the surroundings until I heard a high-pitched whir that was unmistakably the sound of a dental drill. But what was I doing in a dentist's office?

Before I could say something, a figure appeared beside me and looked over me. It was a man's face; his face appeared as a silhouette in the backdrop of the bright white light. He pushed some buttons, and the intensity of the light started to decrease. The mystery dentist was wearing a mask and a lab coat. I winced my eyes and tried to adjust them to the light. As my vision returned, I instantly knew who the masked dentist was.

It was Matty—his hair, his eyes—I could recognize him no matter where I was. I smiled to myself. It was about time I paid a visit to Dr. Oz. He dragged a stool towards the chair and sat on it. As he worked on my teeth, I noticed he was wearing these glasses, magnifying his eyes, and I was constantly staring at them. The wandering eyes stopped abruptly and stared back at me.

"Darlene, I am proud of you, and so is Mike. You are doing really well. Guess what? Mike and I have become buddies. Who would've thought that? Not me."

I just lay there in awe of what was happening. Matty, up close, working on my teeth and talking about befriending my deceased husband. I tried to reply to him a few times but couldn't find any words. He was professionally doing his work. After a while, he stopped, stood, and went away. I stayed where I was.

He returned shortly and pushed another button, angling the dental chair to help me get off it. He gave me his hand to hold on, to help me down. I held it and got off the chair, still staring at him. I then let go of it when my feet touched the floor. As I opened my mouth to thank him, my eyes wandered off to the room we were in, and when I realized where we were, I almost fainted. It was the very same ATM vestibule from the episode where Matty got stuck with Jill Goodacre. But what was I doing there with Oz from the Whole Nine Yards? I woke up before I could turn back to face him and say anything.

The dream felt like one of those crossover episodes. As I am writing this, I am still thinking about it. This might be the greatest start of the year I have ever experienced. I will write more later, trying to process this dream now.

Good Bye Matty

January 2nd, 2024

I am lying in bed, staring at the roof, with Matty's book by my side. I have gone through the first few pages of the book. Whenever I read a sentence, my brain automatically reads it in his voice. This makes me miss him even more.

My brain has memorized Matty's voice so accurately because I love to watch his interviews.

I remember that whenever a new interview was uploaded, I watched that interview every other day. I just love his little mannerisms and the way he emphasizes certain words. But what I loved about those interviews the most was his lightning-quick humor. He had this ability to tell you a story in such a compelling way that it glued you to your screen.

His looks were not the only thing that made me such a fanatic of his. Matty was a master of his craft. He did it with grace and made it look easy. His work on F.R.I.E.N.D.S. contained a lot of his improvisations.

Marta Kaufman and the other writers took his input seriously; his brain was that of a comedic genius. The directors would often add the scene with his improvisations as it would sometimes turn out way more funnier. It's a shame the community didn't recognize his talent with just 5 Emmy nominations. He is on a list of talented actors who have not won an Emmy.

This makes me miss him even more. I can't believe it's been three months since you left me, your FRIENDS, and your fans. In these three months, a lot has happened, but what has remained constant is my hope that this is all a ruse, a sick ruse that has been going on for a long time.

Like a moth to a flame, I am clinging to this idea that you have not gone. You are still with us, somewhere hidden from the limelight, from the cold eyes of the paparazzi who would hound you wherever you went.

From the so-called magazine and their editors who would post pictures of you in unflattering situations and those writers who would constantly remind you of your painful struggle with substance abuse. Or would post before and after comparisons of your appearance. Not even thinking for a moment about how insensitive it is to constantly remind a person about the shadows of his past, which, in some way, haunted him to the last breath that he drew.

Matty, I miss you. When I saw you in the ATM vestibule as Dr Oz, I felt I was on cloud nine. I am still a little dazed by what I saw. I would love to experience this dream once again. Your dreamy blue eyes pierced through my soul. As a woman of faith, I believe that we have to return to our Creator sooner or later. I remember when Mike died. It was a very sad day. I was totally devastated. I was numb with shock, but still, I dragged myself through the Eulogy.

I remember as I spoke, it felt as if countless needles were poking me in my heart. The pain was unbearable. My soulmate was lying there peacefully in his coffin, his last resting place. I cried a lot. I prayed that such a day would never occur in my life ever again. But God had other plans. Two years later, I was living the worst day of my life again.

Oh Matty, when you died, I felt this familiar rush of emotions and the familiar weight on my chest, which made it difficult to breathe. I remember October 28th clearly. My head was spinning violently.

Similarly, I am writing your Eulogy just like the one I wrote for Mike. The only difference was that the funeral lasted for a day. But yours is the one that is ever going. I really miss you, Matty.

There isn't a day that goes by when I don't think about you. The wounds that you have inflicted on my life and my soul are enormous. No matter how much I try to heal, your memories keep resurfacing, stirring my mind and testing my soul.

My healing process is a long road, one that is not linear. Matty, I want you to be with me while I heal, visit me in my dreams, talk to me, make jokes most importantly, support me. Your demise has crushed me into pieces. Help me collect myself.

2:00

I was going through my phone and came across a photo of Matty that I had saved. I absolutely love this expression! He did it a lot! It just looks so mischievous!! How could you say no to that face? You were so gorgeous!

Miss you every day.

Will always love you!!

January 28ᵗʰ , 2024

3 Months...three months without your smiling face...three months without those beautiful eyes. I can't believe it's been three months since you left us. To your family and your Friends Friends that are grieving this horrible loss that just happened way too soon, please know that all of his loving fans grieve as well. Every day gets just a little easier, but it will never be the same without you in this world. Your work that you took such pride in is still being accomplished every day. It hurts so much that you suffered alone all those years. I hope you know what kind of impact you made on this world. Rest in Peace "Matty" you will always be in my dreams. #ripmatthewperry #endlesslove 😢💜💜

This is the message I just posted on my socials. It has been precisely three months since Matty drew his last breath. When I think of the way he died, all alone in the hot tub at his house, I get very emotional. Almost instantly, I start tearing up. I think about the fact that it has been three months, and the pain of his demise still hurts me as much as it did in October. I have been quite inactive for some time, at least in journaling my thoughts. My routine has been pretty much the same. I fall asleep watching Matty every night. The only difference lately was that I could not bring myself to write anything.

Whenever I held the pen, a wave of sadness encapsulated me; it was the type of sadness that renders a person unable to think straight, and the only thing I could do in that state was cry. For the past three weeks or so, my healing process has taken a severe hit.

Oh, Matty, I really miss you. Sometimes, I wish the Lord would have taken me instead of you. That would have been great. The end of Darlene would have been a very quiet one. No Breaking News and no headlines. By now, Darlene would have been forgotten by the world. More importantly, you would have been alive, working on yourself and fighting your demons. Trying to be the best version of yourself for your own sake but for the millions that call themselves your fans.

As for Darlene, she would have perished peacefully, and along with her, she would have perished the memories and admiration she had for this blue-eyed actor with a razor-sharp wit. Buried with her would be the passion that burns deep in her heart.

6:00

As I was going over what I had written earlier, it hit me the amount of influence that Matty's death had on me. I had never wished death upon me before ever in my life, not even when Mike died.

When Michael died, I was shocked beyond comprehension. The first few weeks after his death were very challenging. When the shock wore off, the sadness took its place. It felt like every ounce of happiness and joy inside my body disappeared. I didn't know what could be done to remedy my situation. Over time, I came to a realization. The inevitability of death is a hazardous phenomenon lurking in the shadows. Like a seasoned predator, it attacks its prey immensely, leaving it dumbfounded.

Slowly but surely, I found my footing back. I started feeling like my old self again. By the third month (if my memory serves me right), I started living my life again, knowing he had gone to a better place than this cruel world. The credit goes to my family and, to some extent, Matty, as they supported me in my darkest times. From then on, whenever I think about Michael, I picture him strolling in the meadows of Paradise in a white outfit. I smile whenever this image flashes before my eyes.

Come to think of it, Michael's absence might be the reason for my reaction to your demise. If Michael were here, he would've done his very best to support me. He understood me like no one. My family blesses them. They are as supportive as possible, but I don't understand the bond you and I shared, Matty! They don't know why I would be so sad at the death of a celebrity with whom I have never had any relation, nor had I met him in person.

Only my Mike would have known. He would have supported me, embraced me, and consoled me in every way that he would've known. Part of the blame for my condition can be attributed to my routine. From the moment I wake up to the moment I close my eyes, if there is something that I do as consistently as breathing, it is remembering Matty. But that is something that I can't stop doing. For the better part of ten years, I have been unable to sleep without watching an interview or an episode of Friends.

My admiration for Matty as a person and an artist has adversely impacted my healing process. Another reason might be my blatant refusal to accept the fact that you died in the initial stages of my healing process. The physical aspect of the funeral might come into play as well. I was at the funeral. I delivered, well stammered Eulogy. I saw the coffin, and I kissed him goodbye. I was present when he was buried in the cemetery, and I finally placed the first red rose on his grave.

With Matty, it was a completely different ball game. I was in the living room thinking about how I would decorate my porch for Halloween. At about 10, my phone started blowing up. These were the notifications of the countless Matthew Perry fan pages I had followed. I read the news and couldn't believe what the screen displayed. Initially, I played it off as a rumor or a bandwagon of trolls spreading misinformation. After I did my due diligence, I felt my head spin. I couldn't believe what I was reading. It was on that fateful night my painful voyage started. I'll write more later. Till then, goodbye. Miss you, Matty.

February 4th, 2024

He appeared in my dream again!!

It had been a long time since he made an appearance in my dreams. I was longing to see him with my eyes closed. A part of me was happy as whenever he visited my dreams, it led me to lose my head. I thought about it day and night tirelessly. The better word to use would be overthink, yeah.

I dedicated a copious amount of my time to overanalyzing every detail and trying to remember every nook and cranny of the dream. But the other side that usually prevailed in the internal tussle that took place inside my head wanted Matty to visit me in my sleep.

In all honesty, even I was curious to see how he'd appear this time. His last appearance as Oz from the Whole Ten Yards captivated me in such a manner that I was left wanting more. To improve my chances of getting a visit, I doubled the dose of Vitamin P.

I watched a staggering amount of videos that revolved around Matty. Whether it be a video, an interview, a backstage blooper, or the actual episode, I watched it and sometimes even rewatched it. This whole process left me extremely exhausted by the time I got to bed. As soon as I hit the bed, it was lights out for poor Darlene.

I followed this regime for three consecutive days, and on the third night, he came back. As soon as an episode of FRIENDS finished, I could feel myself being encapsulated in a tsunami wave of drowsiness, so much so that my phone slipped out of my hand and landed safely but painfully on my nose. In a state of extreme drowsiness, I got ready for bed, and as soon as my head hit the soft pillow, I was off to dreamland. Hoping I wouldn't be alone this time.

I found myself in a park. It was one of those parks that had grassy inclines. Due to the elevated position of the park you could see the whole city from there. It was absolutely majestic. As I looked around, I saw a figure sitting on a bench, lost in deep thoughts. He had his back towards me. I knew right away who that man was. Slowly, I approached the bench, and as I was right behind the man. He spoke without moving.

"I was expecting you, Darlene. It has been quite some time since we had our last meeting."

His voice made me grin ear to ear. A warmth filled up my body. I felt so light and airy that if I had flapped my hands, I would have flown away with the flock of birds that were flying above us.

I walked meekly up to the bench and sat beside him. He was wearing a beige colored Oxford jacket and grey pants. He was wearing a white dress shirt that was neatly tucked inside his pants and purple tie. He looked so handsome in the outfit that I took my time to eye him from head to toe. His gray hair was neatly styled, lightly blowing away in the wind. He was wearing one of those clear-frame glasses that tied the whole outfit together. Seeing him so put together warmed my heart.

He was sitting there silently, enjoying the light breeze and soaking up the elements. He closed his eyes and leaned back. At that moment, he was in such a peaceful state that I decided not to bother him. I sat there and just observed him. After what seemed like an eternity (I don't know how to read the time in dreamland). He straightened up and opened up his eyes. Brandishing the icy blues, he looked at me, and I felt as if the air in my lungs vanished.

He then smiled at me and pointed in a direction. I turned to see what he was pointing towards and saw a street. To my surprise, it was the infamous street outside Central Perk café. What shocked me even more was the fact that the "Friends" were all standing on the curb outside the café. They were all young and energetic. But that's not all; I gasped loudly when I saw the young Chandler there as well. He was joking around with Joey and Ross. As I turned around to ask what was going on, Matty had vanished in thin air.

I looked around and even called him out. But to no avail. He had once again snubbed me. Despite being that up and close, I was unsuccessful in talking to him. I turned around to the café and saw that Chandler had stopped joking with his other friends and looking directly towards me. The way his eyes were positioned precisely in my direction told me that it was no fluke. What happened next confirmed it: he kept his gaze on me, smiled, and nodded in a way that showed that he acknowledged my existence.

As I was about to wave back to him, my alarm clock brought me back to the real world—the realm of melancholy. I woke up and immediately started writing. It has been an hour since then. I have written anything and everything that I remember of last night.

I will write later now. A bagel or two might be the greatest thing in the world right now.

Good Bye

Love You Matty

7:00

I was reading an article today about the healing process. It stated that sharing your pain with the concerned community might help you with the healing process. After thinking about it for a while, I have concluded that there are people who are still mourning the death of Matty, just like me. I have decided to open a social media group that would help us share our stories and how Matty impacted our lives. Will put my plans into action by tomorrow

February 5ᵗʰ ,2024

After much contemplation, I have decided to set up a group to connect with people around the world who feel the same as I do about you. It would be a Facebook group. I haven't decided on a name yet.

What I know is that it would have your name. I am very excited about this venture. I want to find others like me who are as passionate as I am about you. It would be great to create a community where people across the world can come together and share their feelings with each other.

I have been following a lot of fan groups. When I communicate with the other followers, it gives me a sense of belonging. I need it now more than ever. Opening up a group would allow me to share the pain that has been inside my heart for the past five months. I try my best to journal every day.

But every now and then, overwhelming waves of sadness take over my mind, and I drown deep in sorrow. This forces me to take a sabbatical from writing. I need to rethink my strategy. I need to go out there and find like-minded people with whom I can share my feelings. I need to listen to the stories of others. I need to get inspired.

Surely, it would take time to heal. A part of me would never be the same at all, but I am ready to embrace reality. I need to accept the fact that you are no longer among us. You have left this world. What's left behind are your memories. Memories that should be cherished. With this group, I aim to curate your memories in digital form. This group would go beyond me. A platform for your fans where they can congregate and remember you.

It will also help me with the loneliness and, after a very long time, give me a sense of purpose in my life. Oh Matty, even in your passing you are helping me out to be a better person.

I just need to find a name for it, and then I will be all set. I recently watched the Good Wife TV series; I absolutely loved him in the role of Mike Kresteva. You show your acting chops in this series by playing the antagonist.

Even though you only appeared for an episode or two and were gone once, your arc ended. I would have loved for you to stay as a regular character. You looked very handsome in your dark grey suit, and that blood-red tie really brought the blue of your eyes. I have screenshotted that still and will use that in one of my posts.

I am excited for what's to come ahead. I will write more later.

8:00

Why can't people let other people live peacefully?

I am writing this after a long and painful interaction I had online with a person. I was watching a video edit of you, Matty. It had clips from the funeral episode from the first season. You looked so dashing in that episode. I am sad to the core, but I remember what you were wearing: a black overcoat with a red scarf and sunglasses.

When I opened the comments section to read what people had written, I was shocked. The very first comment was a horrible joke about your addictions. The comment took me aback.

I am no stranger to trolls who write anything to garner ten seconds of attention and some cheap laughs at other's expense. But what I came across today was such a harsh and cruel joke that too aimed at a person who is no longer among us. Acting against my better judgment, I confronted the troll. Using up all my literary prowess, I formulated a well-written paragraph that criticized the actions of the troll. Just as I hit send, I realized my mistake. I had given the troll the very thing he desired, a reaction that too of a vast magnitude.

As the anger left my body, I felt a similar wave of sadness. Here I was again at ground zero, crying, feeling absolutely weak. All the energy that I had in the morning had been drained. Oh, Matty, why can't people be as kind as you were? I really miss you,

As I lay on the bed, I felt my phone's notifications going wild. It made me remember the dreadful night. My phone was going off similarly. After some contemplation, I decided I would take these trolls head-on. I won't back down and defend my Matty against their vile japes. I was ready to rumble. But as I opened my phone, I was astonished, flabbergasted would be a better word. I saw dozens of fans supporting me. As I went through the comments, I felt warm. I had tears in my eyes, but this time. They were tears of joy, not sorrow. And one comment particularly caught my eye. It said

Have some faith, will you? You don't bad mouth the dead

I had my EUREKA! Moment. I knew what my group would be called. It would be called Matthew Perry – Faithful Fans.

Now, I know it is not that fancy, but it has meaning. It will remind me of this event and, in its own peculiar way, has affected my faith positively. It has taught me to find light in the darkest moment and to never lose hope. I feel like I should thank the trolls as well. If they hadn't done what they did, I would still be scratching my head looking for a name. Now that the name is decided, I will make the group tomorrow and start posting. I hope I find the "faithful fans" that I want to connect with. I should probably get some rest now. Tomorrow will be a busy day. As always

Good Bye
Love You Matty

February 7ᵗʰ ,2024

Today is the first day of the Matthew Perry Faithful Fans. I was thinking about what should be the first post of the group. I want to write something that is sincere and comes from within my heart. All I know is that I want to pour my heart and soul into this project. I hope that through this group, your fans get the necessary help to ease their grieving process.

Last week was rough for me. I found myself going backwards in my healing process. I know this happens, but it's still hard. I miss your smiling face and those beautiful blue eyes! My hope is that you now understand the impact you made on so many. We are comforted in the fact that you are now healed and at peace. But for us here, it still hurts. Forever love! #endlesslove #ripmatty 🖤

This is what I wrote today. I feel this will resonate with others who are still struggling to process your death. Even more I am really excited to communicate with like-minded individuals—those who are as passionate about you, Matty, as I am.

I have started downloading any and every picture of yours that I have come across. I will use them in my posts. One thing I have noticed while going through the photographs is that you look different in almost all of them. In some, you wear your hair longer, and in some, you wear it shorter. There are some where you look slim, and in others, you look bulky. There are some in which you have facial hair, and in others you are clean-shaven. Every picture has a story behind it that displays where you were at that specific time of life.

And I want to discuss those moments with people who are as captivated as I am about you. Oh, Matty, I am really excited about it. But it makes me miss you even more. It's a bittersweet moment for me as I feel good about engaging myself in this project. Even in your death, you helped me, helped me be the better version of myself. If only you would return in my dreams. I have so much to tell you. I never get to talk to you in the "cameos" that you make in my dreams. I just hope the right people find the group, I want to share your legacy with as many as possible. Doing that would help me in my grieving process. I think this is a step in the right direction. I finally found the purpose that I was seeking in my life after retirement. When Mike passed away, he took with him my drive to explore. For a long time, it felt as if I had buried my propensity to try new things along with him. This venture is proving my theory wrong. All that poor Mike took with himself was the happiness and the warm fuzzy feeling that I had when we talked or when we went for long walks on the beach. I feel sad when I reminisce about the good old days. A bombardment of emotions is going on inside my head. I feel happy, sad, nostalgic, excited, amused and a lot more than what mere words could explain. I will write later. I feel overwhelmed right now.

7:00

I just checked the group, and guess what? I got some likes, and heart reacts. Along with that some kind comments about you, Matty. This is working just as I thought it would. I have found a platform where I can express my admiration for you. There are some who have joined the group and posted some messages and pictures as well. Didn't I tell you, Matty? That there would be people as devoted as me. I would just love for this community to grow and prosper.

To better understand the enigma you were, I have decided to read your book. I got it way back when it was released, but I was unable to get myself to read it. I have got myself the audio version as well to make it easier to go through. I have heard positive reviews about the book. I am eager to post more. Let's see what the future holds for the Mathew Perry – Faithful Fans group.

I will write later on. Till then, as always, Good Bye, Love You, Matty

February 28ᵗʰ ,2024

Friends, Lovers and The Big Terrible Thing, you wrote this book about your life, and although you have been in our living rooms and bedrooms for 30 years now, we did not know you. Why, Matty, did you not let us know you were suffering? I have never met you, but after listening to your book about twelve times now I feel I could have carried on a conversation like we have known each other for years. As it turns out, we had a lot in common. You certainly like a view which I have always dreamed of having and you just want to sit on the couch and watch movies. These are just a couple of things that we had in common. You were handsome, funny and certainly "Enough". We are so sad that we did not know until your memoir came out. I miss you so much. We are healing, but it will take a while. You left us way too soon. I love and miss you every day, but you are now healed and at peace. #endlesslove #ripmatty🖤☺

For the past two weeks or so, I have been extremely busy with the group, posting, reacting and talking with your fans. I have completed your book in the audio version and have started to read it as well. I just posted this. Safe to say, what I knew about you was just the tip of the iceberg. There is so much to your story, so much to your life than jokes and sketches. We all knew that he had his struggles with substance abuse, just like many other stars in the showbiz industry.

But never would have I ever thought that he experienced such darkness. In the first chapter of the book, he recounts the near-death experience that he had, and the details took me aback. Oh, Matty, going through this book really made me understand how ambiguous the term "struggle" is. Behind those smiles was a man who had gone through horrible events. My admiration for you has increased tenfold.

March 17ᵗʰ ,2024

It's Sunday...lonely weekend thinking about Matty. I find it getting easier to deal with. Watching him every day in one thing or another helps a lot. I will never forget you, nor stop loving you! Still miss you every day! I know he's watching over us and understands how we all feel! Love you Matty #ripmatty 🖤🖤

It's a Sunday, and I have just woke up. Last night I watched Growing Pains where you play the role of Sandy. I recently came upon the fact that Matty had a brief role in the sitcom Growing Pains. You were so young (just 18), and it radiated from your face. The episode was sad, as your character died at the end due to a DUI accident. Oh, Matty, you looked so handsome in that episode. Despite the melancholic tone of the episode, I love the fact that you portrayed your character. When Carol visits you at the hospital. Despite your injuries and grievances, you joke with her. I really miss you today, Matty. For the past two weeks, I have been busy with the group. It has started garnering an audience. Over the weeks, I have had great conversations with great people. It absolutely warms my heart to talk with them and share my love for you with them.

I am happy to have found my corner on the World Wide Web. I consider these people essential for my healing process. When I talk with them and read their posts, I feel elevated. It shields me from the waves of sadness, which I have so very often written about.

I love spending hours and hours on the group, it makes me proud to have crafted a platform that others can use to express their feelings. I will write more later.

Good Bye

Love You Matty

March 20ᵗʰ ,2024

As I lie in bed this morning, waking way too early I was thinking of you, Matty! All of these thoughts went through my mind, so wanted your passing to be a dream and it wouldn't be true that you are gone. We miss you so much! Your struggles were real and we so wish you didn't have to go through them. There are ugly things being said about you. How dare they attack you when you can't defend yourself! I choose not to believe. So I am posting pics that you have a big smile on your face because this is the way I remember you! I love you forever and miss you deeply! #endlesslove #ripmatty 👑

This is what I posted today.

I'm not particularly eager to use the word hate. It is such a terrible word and an emotion that I refrain from utilizing. But I am at my wit's end. I am talking about the people who are writing vile things about you, Matty. I usually try to ignore the trolls who try to achieve their five seconds of fame. While I ignore them as much as I could. But cruel jokes and comments slandering a dead man boil my blood. I hate these people from the bottom of my heart. Oh, Matty, they do not know about the struggles that you have gone through. They do not care about the painful days and nights that you have suffered. All they care about is having a laugh at the expense of the tragedy of a dead man.

Oh, Matty, The group is a blessing in disguise. It acts as a sanctuary for me where I can express my thoughts. I have been disturbed by the insults hurled at your name. I will rest now and write later on.

Good Bye

Love You Matty

March 27ᵗʰ ,2024

It's a gray day, and I'm missing you terribly! Just finished your audiobook for the 15th time. The last two chapters are the hardest to take. I get so sad that you finally figured out life, and it was taken away! From the "big terrible thing" that you went through to living life without alcohol, drugs and smoking, I so wish I could have helped you through it all. I would have never left you alone, EVER! It's all water under the bridge now, but I miss you so bad. I'm keeping you alive through your amazing legacy of work. #endlesslove #ripmatty 😈

I have been under the weather for some days. But no worries, I have you with me. I listened to your audiobook again. Your voice works wonders for me.

March 28ᵗʰ ,2024

Lord is Great!!! You came back after a long time in my dream. I have just woken up and feel I should record the details. I dozed off while listening to the audiobook. There I was in pitch-black darkness, and my body felt as if it was floating in the air. I started hearing a faint voice. Keep in mind it was still pitch black. After concentrating, I was dead sure whose voice it was. I felt the voice getting louder, as if it was coming towards me. As the voice got louder and closer, the atmosphere was getting cooler and brighter. As I adjusted my eyes to the sudden surge of brightness in the place I was, I noticed a figure, and to my delight, it was you, Matty.

You were wearing a white shirt and jeans and were sporting a salt-and-pepper beard. You had your book in hand and swaggered towards me. With the electric blues fixated on me, you sit nearby and start reading the book. I just kept looking at you, too stunned to say anything. Unfortunately, that was all while listening to your voice. I dozed off in my dream and ended up in the realm of reality as I looked at the calendar. I realized it was the 28th of March. How could I forget this fateful date? The 28th of every month would take me back to October 2023; I was in my bedroom figuring out how to decorate my house for Halloween. When, all of a sudden, my phone started going off, just like that you were gone, away from our lives. To commemorate this, I posted this.

5 months, It's five months since you left us! I'm missing you just as much today as the day you went home to glory. Matty, I want you to know that the legacy you hoped for has happened and is doing unbelievable work. But this does not change how we feel about you. I miss you everyday Matty! My heart hurts for you. We will do our best to keep your legacy alive! Each day gets a tiny bit easier but I still hurt. Love you always! #endlesslove #ripmatty 🫶 💀🖤

April 1ˢᵗ, 2024

"April Fools!!!!"

I heard a noise while I was watering my plants. When I turned around, I saw two kids that lived down the block. One of them was laughing his heart out. The other stood quiet, amazed, slightly amazed at his naivety. I was standing in the front of my lawn with a garden hose, enjoying this interaction. I was almost impossible to stop yourself from smiling. Seeing them took me back to my old childhood when I used to play with my friends, and I was quite the prankster in my day.

As I was reminiscing about the good old days. I felt someone put their arm on my shoulder. It was most probably an arm of a man. I was shocked beyond comprehension as I turned my head to see who it was. It was you, Matty!!!

I stayed in that position for a while, trying to make words that had left my mind when I saw you. You stood by me with your arm on my shoulder, smiling, watching those kids chase each other. The sun's rays bounced off your skin, making you look like an angel. The next thing I knew, one of the kids started running in our direction. As he reaches near us, he tries to hug Matty, who vanishes in thin air. I then hear a sound. The alarm clock that brought me back to reality.

Oh, Matty, you have played a trick on me again until the very end; I thought my dream of being with you had finally come true. But alas, it was just one of these dreams that I sometimes have.

I really like them and look forward to your next visit, but it makes me miss you even more. I have just woken up and have started writing. I don't want to miss any details.

7:00

"Monday has come and just about gone. As I sit here at home, I find it lonely. Sometimes, I yearn for a partner again. Matty why did you leave? You had so much more life to live and so many more things to accomplish. Your book has touched so many of us. I know you wrote it to help others like you, but for us who aren't dealing with that terrible thing, we also need to hear it. As I listen to your voice every day, I feel comforted. I miss you sooo much, Matty, that sometimes it hurts. I think it always will, somewhat. I'm not as sad as I was, so please know that healing is coming along. You will forever have a piece of my heart that will want you still here! #endlesslove #ripmatty 💀🖤 "*

This is what I just posted; I really miss you, Matty. I want to honor your memory.

April 4ᵗʰ,2024

I have been under the weather for the past three days or so. I am suffering from a fever and fits of horrible coughs. My throat is very sore. It feels as if someone has scrapped the inside of my throat with a high grit sandpaper. It makes eating food and swallowing drinks extremely painful. In all these hardships, the light in the dark is your presence in my life. Whenever I feel weak or defeated, I remind myself of the words that you said when you visited me in one of my dreams.

I have been watching the earlier seasons of F.R.I.E.N.D.S. It is one of the greatest comforts in my life. It warms my heart and gives me joy. My group gives me strength. The conversations that I had for the past two days made me feel better. The way they showered me with well-wishes cemented the fact that, indeed, this group was more than just a fan group.

We nurture unity and positivity and try to elevate each other. This group has proven to be what I wanted: a platform for those who want to express their feelings.

"Thursday, and I'm kinda blue. Something happened that I'm not going to discuss, but when I look at this face, all my problems melt away! Matty how do you do it? Love you and miss you so bad it really hurts right now. You put up with a lot during your too short life. You went through hell trying to find your way. Your beautiful blue eyes and face help me tonight! Tomorrow is another day, and it will be great! Thank you, Matty, for being you!! #endlesslove #ripmatty 😢😭🖤"

After this post, numerous people came forward via messages to check up on me, and that made me feel really good. It is truly my privilege to gather like-minded people who care for each other. Oh, Matty, it would not have been possible without you.

May 5th ,2024

It's the 5th of May. My healing process has really taken a nose dive; here I was, taking baby steps towards recovery. When all of a sudden. I fell ill at the start of the month. Even though I have recovered by the grace of God, I feel as if the episode of illness has evaporated all the happiness that I had gathered so painstakingly. Along with that, it took away my will to write. After a long time, I have felt like myself, so I would devote this time towards the group; below is the post that I wrote today :

"Sitting here on a Thursday, watching your beautiful blue eyes on Studio 60! They had a lot of close-ups in this series, so I love seeing his face! There have been so many pictures of you at your best and worst. Unfortunately, that's a part of being a celebrity. It doesn't make it right, though. You had so many highs and lows in your life, and it makes me sad! Especially since you were alone for the majority of it! All of your fans are sick about this, and any one of us would have helped you through this loneliness and loved you endlessly! We still love you endlessly! Matty, I'm so sorry you had to go through this alone! You are at peace now and you know how much we loved you and again still do! Pics today are among some of my favorites that you are so beautiful in. Let's "Celebrate Him" #endlesslove #ripmatty 🤍💀🖤"

May 11ᵗʰ,2024

It's Mother's Day. I saw a program about mothers who had lost their sons, and almost immediately, my mind went to Suzanne, your mom, and Matty; I was just thinking about how she was. I have seen her pictures; she is a beautiful lady indeed. I have read about your early childhood and how you felt abandoned, as if you were invisible. You then dwell on how to counter these negative experiences. You had to use humor as a crutch to make your sad life bearable. But I loved the fact that later on in life, you mended bridges with your mother and were successful in having a loving, meaningful relationship with both your mother and your father. This just goes to show what kind of person you were beyond the silver screen. To express this, I posted this:

"Oh, Matty! The first Mother's Day without you! Your mother's heart was already broken. But today, it's even harder. You were the one who made her a mother, and she will forever remember you. Even in the hard times that you had, I know deep down your love for your mother was there! When you needed her in your younger years, she didn't quite get it, but she turned it around and loved you to the end! A mother should never have to bury a child. It's just too hard! Like Matty, I never became a parent, but I understand the love. She and we miss you every day! #endlesslove #ripmatty 💜💜"

I will write later

Good Bye

Love You Matty

May 18ᵗʰ,2024

I know I've written about this before, but I just watched the movie "Numb" again. I honestly do not know how Matty made this movie! It had to be so triggering in so many ways. The scene with his mother could not have been any harder. Although it had to be easy to express hisself in this scene. I found myself very sad watching parts, knowing what he went through in his life. Even though he came out on the right side in real life. I want to end this entry on a good note. He looked so bright and happy in recent years. If you have a chance to watch this movie Matty's acting was outstanding! "Celebrate Him" #ripmatty 💀🖤

I just saw the movie that a group member suggested to me. It is called "Numb,"

I was blown away by it. It's one of those movies that I had no idea of. I loved your acting in this movie. As I am writing this post, what I realized was that during the shooting of that film you were going through one of the darkest periods of your life. The way you portrayed the character of Hudson Milbank, a man suffering from depersonalization disorder, with so much ease, goes to show that you, yourself, were experiencing harrowing issues in life. With that being said, your acting prowess should not be overlooked as well.

Oh, Matty, I really miss you. It really makes me tear up when I look at your work. The fact that you are no longer with us really makes my heart bleed. I will write later on.

Good Bye

Love You Matty

May 28ᵗʰ ,2024

7 months, it's been 7 months since you left us. I can't believe we've gone seven months without your smiling face and your beautiful eyes. As I sit here watching Studio 60, I'm on the episode where you start writing the show high! These couple of episodes make my heart hurt. How did you do it? I believe you were sober during this run, but these stories had to be very difficult. I get sooo sad watching you. I think about all those times that you sat alone in your home, taking all of those drugs just to feel normal. We will always ask why? You were always enough, you weren't bent or broken. It makes me cry that you thought you weren't good enough for any relationship. I would have loved to sit down and have a conversation with you. To finish I want to send hope that your family is working through their grief. Could not imagine what they are going through. Please know that I will always love and miss you Matty. Watch over us for now! #endlesslove #ripmatty 😢💜

Oh, Matty, It has been seven months since you left me and joined heaven. But it feels as if it was just yesterday. The wound that your painful demise has caused on my soul has not healed yet. Part of the wound would never heal up, I feel. As long as my tears flow and my heart beats, I will never forget you. Your killer smile and dashing eyes are etched on my brain.

June 2ⁿᵈ ,2024

I have been too busy to write and have been planning and preparing for a trip to Las Vegas for my retirement. Yes, I have retired, and to commemorate this day, I will be going to Vegas. I am really excited and will write more later.

11:00

As I was lying in my hotel, a thought ran into my head: you made Fools Rush In here in Vegas. But this was the place where you got injured, and according to you, this was the place where your problems started. It was this movie where you had a jet ski injury that caused you to take opiates. I suddenly feel extremely sad. Oh, Matty, wherever I go, I feel as if you are with me. I am watching the Vegas episode. After having a great time, I am tired and will sleep now,

"Arrived in Las Vegas yesterday...channeling my inner Matty! Heading to the Grand Canyon today. I plan to have a silent moment in Matty's memory! He made his best movie here. Will be thinking of you all day today. Sometimes, life is cruel, but we know that it was God's plan. You left us way too soon! Love and miss you every day. #endlesslove #ripmatty 🖤💙 *"*

June 10ᵗʰ ,2024

Arrived home safely...had the time of my life, and I'm ready to go again! I channeled Matty a lot on this trip. Thinking of him every time I went to a location where I knew he had been. But back to reality, and you're still gone. I didn't get to listen to your book the whole time I was gone. When I listened to it today, I didn't realize how must I miss you until I heard your voice. Listening to your struggles once again just hurt my heart once again! It hurts so bad to think you went through your struggles alone. I found a Friends treasure at the famous Pawn shop in Vegas. The picture has you with such a great smile. My wish is that it was at a good time in your life. I know you had some! So pics today will once again show your smile that was so beautiful! Miss you and will always love you. #endlesslove #ripmatty 🖤🖤

I had the time of my life during the trip. Oh, Matty, I always remembered you. Throughout the trip, I felt as if you were with me, and I was absolutely right !!! I found a picture of you in a pawn shop. You look so good in that picture that, the way the picture focuses on your eyes. Those bright blue eyes of yours, the eyes that made me fall head over heels when I first saw you. I will sleep now.

Good Bye

Love You Matty

June 15ᵗʰ ,2024

The first Father's Day without you. I can't imagine what your father will go through tomorrow! My prayer is that he is at peace, but he is probably having a really hard day. You were a challenge at times but your father was there for you always. I'm sure he held your hand when you were detoxing all those times. His love for you was so dedicated and deep. I know you loved your father with all your heart. He misses you, Matty! We miss you too! Love you always! Happy Father's Day - #JohnBennettPerry #ripmatty 🐼😿🖤

John Bennet Perry is an actor by profession; while his acting career sadly did not reach the heights that he had wished for, his dreams to achieve superstardom were fulfilled by his son Matthew Perry (Matty for me). I just came across a picture the other day. It was of you, Matty, alongside your dad. I see where you got your handsome looks from. That's all from me today.

Good Bye

Love You Matty

June 28ᵗʰ ,2024

How is it possible that you've been gone 8 months? Our hearts are still hurting. You were such an incredible human being. Your heart was so big and so full of love. You told us that you wanted everyone to talk about how you helped everyone possible beat this disease that you struggled with the majority of your life. You beat this disease down enough that you could live a life without drugs and, alcohol and even smoking! We are so proud of you! These days, in your absence, your name is in the press again. They are close to finding out who gave you the final straw that took you away! I don't know how I feel about this. There is not enough being said! Did you know it was too much? What was really bothering you that you felt the need to take it? We will never know. We can only grieve now! We miss you sooo badly. Every day gets a little easier, and you would be so proud that your legacy will live on forever!! Thank you, Matty, for the memories! #endlesslove #ripmatty 😢😿💜 #ripmatty 😢😿💜

I saw your name pop up in the news today. Apparently, they are opening up an investigation to find out who provided you with ketamine. A substance that you have had struggles with. You were brave enough to come forward and address this issue; your bravery made me respect you even more. As per the reports, I have read that you were going through treatment to get better and allegedly, you overdosed on your medication; I think and cry about it. What were you feeling that day? I am very upset at the crude remarks some people are making of you. I love you and still miss you to this very day. I will write later as I have to run some errands.

July 4th ,2024

It's the 4th of July, and it's a lonely one. I have no plans today, which is really sad. I'm sitting here writing and thinking of you. I've been thinking of you a lot this week. I'm working on a tribute that will honor everything about you, Matty. I think of your family as I work through it and cannot begin to understand the grieving they are experiencing. Your fans are hurting still and maybe we will hurt forever, but the hurt is getting way easier to manage. But still, we love and miss you every day and forever. #endlesslove #ripmatty 💔💜

I sit here watching the fireworks, alone on my lawn. Oh, Matty, how I wish you were here. The other day, I was sitting there and went into a trance-like state. I was dreaming with my eyes open, and I saw a huge field where you and I were sitting by a bonfire toasting marshmallows, watching the fireworks go off. I was brought back into reality when my phone rang.

I will write later till then.

Good Bye

Love You Matty

July 18ᵗʰ ,2024

Coming into the weekend soon. Saturday is always a hard day. Since this is the day we lost you. Going through social media this morning and seeing all the wonderful pictures, videos of you. This just makes me miss you even more! I know that all you ever wanted was to be loved by that special person and to have a family. So sorry you never got that last chapter in your life. Matty, your legacy is living on. Your foundation is thriving, and your TV and film work lives on. Your fans will forever love and miss you. Each day gets a little easier, but our hearts are forever scarred. Rest in peace, dear Matty.

#endlesslove #matthewperrytribute 💜💜

When I was working, I had other things on my plate. I had things that would keep me busy, and my mind would be focused elsewhere despite that. To not only survive but thrive professionally, I had to focus, pushing my memories and my emotions in the back of my head at work (that was the hardest task I did).

All those bottled emotions would overflow when I got home. Many a time, I would enter my house and start crying. These were some of the darkest days of my life. Now that I have retired, I feel more at ease with myself. I don't have to constantly hide my emotions and negate the feelings that I have. Oh, Matty, I miss you, especially on Saturday. October 28ᵗʰ, Saturday, was the day I lost you. After that week, there have been very few Saturdays that I have been truly happy with my life. I will write more later.

Good Bye

Love You Matty

July 21ˢᵗ ,2024

Another day...I thank God for every day I wake up. But sometimes I still can't believe you are no longer here among us. There are good days, and there are bad days. I'm thankful for all of them because I still have the memory of you. Matty, for some reason, I don't think the memory of you will ever fade. I'll never understand how someone you have never met could have such a profound hold on you.

But Matty you do that! As your fans try to regain some form of normalcy, I know you are aware of the hold you have on us. If only you knew this when you were here. You were "Enough," and you were lovable! We miss you every day and always will. Rest easy, dear Matty! #endlesslove #matthewperrytribute 🖤 🖤

As I open my eyes, I get to see your beautiful face. I recently got a poster that I have posted up on my bedroom wall. When you think of it, it might sound silly and almost childish, but ever since I got that poster, I feel a lot more safer and sleep a lot better. Your icy blues make me feel cooler. As I am writing this, I feel blood rush to my cheeks, and I feel a little shy. But that's what I truly feel, so that's what I write. I will write later.

Good Bye

Love You Matty

August 19ᵗʰ, 2024

Happy Birthday!!!! Matty, I have been sick for a long time. I had contracted a throat infection once again. I got a cake baked, and it read.

HBD MATTY!!! COULD YOU BE ANY SWEETER?

October 4ᵗʰ, 2024

I am shaking, and seething after a long time. My healing process was on the right track. I had started feeling good, and for the past month or so, I felt as if the old Darlene was coming back. That was until Yesterday when I saw your name on the news. You were murdered, Matty. You were taken away from us by the one you confided in and trusted to make you better. But now you are at peace; this cruel world will not bother you anymore.

Good Bye Matty,

I Love You

October 14ᵗʰ, 2024

I am struggling to find words. I have been devastated by the news. You could have been alive right now. You were taken away from us due to the negligence of another person. The only silver lining that I can think of from this sad revelation is that it would silence those who bad-mouthed you and made vile remarks. You were trying to get better, and ironically, that is what caused your demise. I will write later.

Good Bye Matty,

I Love You

October 28ᵗʰ, 2024

It was the 28ᵗʰ of October, 2023, when my world got turned upside down. That day, an angel left the world. What he left behind was his legacy and his fond memories. My blue-eyed angel, my Matty

Oh, Matty, I was at Costco the other day. While going through the canned goods aisle, I heard a group of middle-aged women talking about you, Matty. Oh, I was so excited. It brought a smile to my face. You remain in the hearts of the millions. I posted this in your memory:

Monday...One Year Today! This post comes with great sorrow. I can't believe you have been gone a year. So much has happened in the last year. Matty, why did you have to go so young? Why wasn't there someone that could see what was wrong? Why were you home alone? There are so many why's that will never be answered. All I know is that when you went, all of my anticipation of ever meeting you went with it. You were such a light in a dark world. Your smile, your beautiful blue eyes and your great big giving heart made this world a little brighter. We will never know what really happened, but we will miss you for the rest of our lives. We will fight for your justice and keep your legacy alive. Our healing process has begun, but it's hard. I will forever have a piece of my heart missing, but I feel that it's gotten easier to accept your passing. Don't get me wrong, there are still and will always be triggers that will set me back, but that's ok because that's the price of love! Rest now; you are free of your pain, sweet Matty. You will always be loved and missed. "All for Matty." #endlesslove #matthewperrytribute 🖤🖤

My healing process is far from over, but with each day, it moves forward bit by bit. Though the pain of losing you will always linger, deep within me. The love we have for you remains as strong as ever. You will forever be cherished and deeply missed. Rest easy now, dear Matty; you're always in our hearts until we meet again in dreams.

All for Matty.

Made in the USA
Columbia, SC
03 November 2024

45564217R00035